Austin Bearse

Reminiscences of Fugitive-Slave Law Days in Boston

Austin Bearse

Reminiscences of Fugitive-Slave Law Days in Boston

ISBN/EAN: 9783744617949

Printed in Europe, USA, Canada, Australia, Japan

Cover: Foto ©Suzi / pixelio.de

More available books at **www.hansebooks.com**

REMINISCENCES

OF

Fugitive-Slave Law Days

IN BOSTON.

BY AUSTIN BEARSE.

BOSTON:

PRINTED BY WARREN RICHARDSON.

146 FRANKLIN STREET and 149 CONGRESS STREET.

1880.

Landing a fugitive slave at Drake's Wharf, South Boston, from the Yacht "Moby Dick,"
Capt. Austin Bearse, on the night of July 18, 1853.

[Page 34.

REMINISCENCES

OF

Fugitive-Slave Law Days

IN BOSTON.

By Austin Bearse.

PRINTED BY WARREN RICHARDSON,

146 FRANKLIN STREET and 149 CONGRESS STREET.

1880.

MEMBERS OF THE COMMITTEE OF VIGILANCE.

Adams, Charles B.
Adams, George
Alcott, A. Bronson
Allen, Ephraim
Allyne, Joseph W.
Andrew, John A.
Andrews, Erastus
Apthorp, Robert E.
Atkinson, Edward
Atkinson, William P.
Augustus, John
Ayres, John
Barker, Rensalaer
Baxter, Thompson
Bearse, Austin
Bigelow, Dennis
Bishop, Joel P.
Blakemore, William
Blanchard, Joshua P.
Bolles, John A.
Botume, John, Jr.
Bouve, Thomas T.
Bowditch, Henry I.
Bowditch, William I.
Bramhall, Cornelius
Bridge, Jonathan D.
Brimblecom, F.
Brimblecom, F. A.
Browne, John W.
Bryant, David
Bruce, Jeptha C.
Burlingame, Anson
Burrage, Alvah A.

× Cabot, Fred. S.
Capen, Lemuel
Carew, Thomas
Carnes, George W.
Caswell, Lewis E.
Channing, Wm. F.
Channing, William H.
Chase, L. G.
Cheever, George F.
Child, Daniel F.
Childs, Alfred A.
Colver, Nathaniel
Cornell, William M.
Cowing, Cornelius
Crosby, Robert R.
Curtis, John, Jr.
Cushing, Henry D.
Cutter, Abraham E.
Dana, Richard H., Jr.
Danforth, John C.
Davie, Johnson
Davis, Charles G.
Denio, Sylvanus A.
Dodge, George
Dodge, Joshua G.
Downer, Samuel, Jr.
Edmunds, Edward
Eldridge, John S.
Ellis, Charles
Ellis, Charles M.
Emmons, John L.
Fay, Emery B.
Fillebrown, Edward

FISHER, GEORGE J.
FITCH, JONAS
FULLER, RICHARD F.
GAGE, BENJAMIN W.
GARRISON, WILLIAM LLOYD
GIBBS, JOHN B.
GILBERT, TIMOTHY
GORE, JOHN C.
GOVE, JOHN
GOOCH, DANIEL W.
GREENE, BENJAMIN H.
HAMLET, WILLIAM
HANSCOM, SIMON P.
HANSON, MOSES P.
HAYDEN, LEWIS
HAYES, JOSEPH K.
HERSEY, NATHAN W.
HILDRETH, RICHARD
HILTON, JOHN T.
HOLMAN, JOSHUA B.
HOLMES, RICHARD
HOLMES, WILLIAM H.
HOOD, RICHARD
HOUGHTON, GEORGE W.
HOWE, SAMUEL G.
HOWLAND, DAVID
HOVEY, CHARLES F.
HOXIE, TIMOTHY W.
HUNT, EBENEZER
HUNTER, THOMAS
JACKSON, EDMUND
JACKSON, E. W.
JACKSON, FRANCIS
JAMESON, WILLIAM H.
JENKINS, WILLIAM H.
JEWETT, JOHN P.
KEMP, HENRY
KENDALL, STEPHEN B.

KIMBALL, JOHN S.
KIMBALL, PETER
KING, JOHN G.
KING, T. STARR
KNAPP, FREDERICK N.
LAWTON, JOHN T.
LAYTON, JOSEPH J.
LEWIS, ENOCH
LEWIS, JOEL W.
LINCOLN, HENRY W.
LIST, CHARLES
LLOYD, SAMUEL H.
LOCKE, AMOS W.
LORING, ELLIS GRAY
LOWELL, JAMES RUSSELL
MACKAY, T. B.
MANLEY, JOHN R.
MARJORAM, WILLIAM W.
MARSH, BELA
MARSTON, RUSSELL
MAY, FREDERICK W. G.
MAY, JOHN J.
MAY, SAMUEL, Jr.
MCCREA, J. B.
MCPHAIL, ANDREW M, JR.
MERRIAM, E. S.
MERRILL, GEORGE
MINOT, GEORGE
MITCHELL, GEORGE H.
MOODY, LORING
MORRIS, ROBERT
MUSSEY, BENJAMIN B.
NICHOLS, HENRY P.
NASH, NATHANIEL C.
NELL, WILLIAM C.
ORNE, OTIS
OSGOOD, ISAAC
PARKER, HENRY T.

Parker, Theodore
Parkman, John
Parks, Luther, Jr.
Perkins, Thomas C.
Phelps, Sylvester
Phillips, Wendell
Pratt, J.
Prentiss, Henry J.
Putnam, Joseph H.
Quimby, J. P.
Quincy, Edmund
Raymond, Wm. T.
Richards, James B.
Ritchie, Uriah
Rogers, George M.
Rogers, John S.
Rogers, Robert B.
Russell, George R.
Russell, Thomas, Jr.
Sargent, John T.
Sawyer, Wm. N.
Sewall, Samuel E.
Shaw, Francis G.
Slack, Charles W.
Smilie, J. H.
Smith, Chauncey
Smith, Joshua B.
Smith, J. W.
Smith, Stephen
Snowden, Isaac H.
Southwick, Joseph
Sparrell, William
Spear, John M.
Spooner, Lysander

Spooner, William B.
Steele, William M.
Stone, James W.
Stone, Milton J.
Storrs, Amariah
Sullivan, John W.
Swift, John L.
Taft, A. C.
Talbot, S. D.
Tappan, Charles
Thayer, David
Thompson, John
Tolman, James
Towne, William B.
Treanor, Barnard S.
Trafton, Mark
Trask, Henry P.
Wakefield, Enoch H.
Wallcutt, Robert F.
Walker, Dana D.
Warren, Washington
Waters, Edwin F.
Waterston, Robert C.
Webb, Seth, Jr.
Whipple, Charles K.
White, William A.
Whitman, William H.
Wilson, Alexander
Withington, Oliver W.
Wright, Albert J.
Wright, Elizur
Yerrinton, J. M. W
York, Jasper H.

OFFICERS AND COMMITTEES.

President,	. . .	TIMOTHY GILBERT.
Secretary,	. . .	CHARLES LIST.
Treasurer,	. . .	FRANCIS JACKSON.

EXECUTIVE COMMITTEE.

THEODORE PARKER,   WENDELL PHILLIPS,
JOSHUA B. SMITH,   EDMUND JACKSON,
LEWIS HAYDEN,   CHARLES M. ELLIS,
SAMUEL G. HOWE,   CHARLES K. WHIPPLE.

FINANCE COMMITTEE.

ROBERT E. APTHORP,   JOHN A. ANDREW,
HENRY I. BOWDITCH,   ELLIS GRAY LORING,
WILLIAM W. MARJORAM,   ROBERT MORRIS,
SAMUEL E. SEWALL,   FRANCIS JACKSON.

REMINISCENCES.

THIS publication is dictated by the quick-hearted sympathy of my anti-slavery friend, Rev. PHOTIUS FISK, chaplain United States Navy, who in the best spirit of his native land, classic Greece, has reared appropriate monumental stones to commemorate the deeds of martyrs who have suffered in several States of America for aiding the escape of slaves from galling bondage.

At Mount Auburn, to Rev. CHARLES T. TORREY, who died in a Baltimore jail; at New Bedford, to Captain DRAYTON, who endured a terrible imprisonment for years in Washington — for which Charles Sumner wrote the inscription; at Lake Harbor, Michigan, to Captain JONATHAN WALKER, who, in 1844 was cast into a dungeon, and pierced in the hand with a hot iron, by Florida slaveholders — the hero of Whittier's soul-stirring verse, " *The Branded Hand.*" All Massachusetts citizens,

> " Breasting the full tide of wrong,
> Unappalled by the danger, the shame, and the pain,
> And counting each trial for Truth as their gain."

So, in the slight record of these pages, gratefully dedicated to THE COMMITTEE OF VIGILANCE, would this lover of his fellowmen seek to keep green the memory of the faithful service done to humanity in Boston harbor and streets, in which hunted fugitive slaves were snatched from kidnappers, sheltered, housed and fed, and forwarded with all speed and secrecy to Canada; their rescuers defended in the courts of prosecution, and when Sims and Burns fell victims, their cause plead with unexampled eloquence, till Freedom's fame found wings on every wind.

When, in 1853, Mrs. Harriet Beecher Stowe came to the *Liberator* Office, 21 Cornhill, to get facts for her "Key to Uncle Tom's Cabin," she was taken by Mr. R. F. Wallcutt and myself over to Lewis Hayden's house in Southac Street, where thirteen newly-escaped slaves of all colors and sizes were brought into one room for her to see. Though Mrs. Stowe had written her wonderful "Uncle Tom" at the request of Dr. Bailey, of Washington, for *The National Era*, expressly to show up the workings of the Fugitive-Slave Law, yet she had never seen such a company of "fugitives" together before. Mr. Lewis Hayden was himself a remarkable fugitive slave, whose story Mrs. Stowe introduced in her "Key." She also drew from me the narrative here copied from page 154 of the "Key," prefaced with this notice:

"The following communication has been given to the writer by Captain Austin Bearse. Mr. Bearse is a native of Barnstable, Cape Cod. He is well known to our Boston citizens and merchants."

I am a native of the State of Massachusetts. Between the years of 1818 and 1830, I was from time to time mate on board of different vessels engaged in the coasting trade on the coast of South Carolina. It is well known that many New England vessels are in the habit of spending their winters on the Southern coast, in pursuit of this business — for vessels used to run up the rivers for the rough rice and cotton of the plantations, which we took to Charleston. We often carried gangs of slaves to the plantations as they had been ordered. These slaves were generally collected by slave-traders in Charleston, brought there by various causes, such as the death of owners and the division of estates, which threw them into the market. Some were sent as punishment for insubordination, or because the domestic establishment was too large ; or because persons moving to the North and West preferred selling their slaves to the trouble of carrying them. We had on board our vessels, from time to time, numbers of these slaves — sometimes two or three, and sometimes as high as seventy or eighty. They were separated from their families and connections with as little concern as calves and pigs are selected out of a lot of domestic animals. Our vessel used to lie at a place called Poor Man's Hole, not far from the city. We used to allow the relatives and friends of the slaves to come on board and stay all night with their friends, before the vessel sailed. In the morning it used to be my business to pull off the hatches and warn them that it was time to separate, and the shrieks and cries at these times were enough to make anybody's heart ache. In the year 1828, while mate of the brig "Milton," of Boston, bound from Charleston, S. C., to New Orleans, the following incident occurred, which I shall never forget. The traders brought on board four quadroon men in handcuffs. An old negro woman, more than eighty years of age, came screaming after them, "My son! Oh, my son!" She seemed almost frantic, and when we had got more than a mile out in the harbor, we heard her screaming yet. When we were in the Gulf Stream, I came to the men and took off their handcuffs. They were resolute fellows, and they told me I would see they would never live to be slaves in New Orleans. One of them was a carpenter and one a blacksmith. We brought them into New Orleans, and consigned them over to the agent. The agent told the captain that in forty-eight hours afterwards they were all dead men, having every one killed himself as they said they should. One of them I know was bought for a fireman on the steamer "Post Boy," that went down to the Balize. He jumped overboard and was drowned.

There was a plantation at Coosahatchie, back of Charleston, kept by a widow lady who owned eighty negroes. She sent to Charleston and bought a quadroon girl, very nearly white, for her son. We carried her up. She was more delicate than the other slaves, so she was not put with them, but carried up in the cabin.

I have been on the rice plantations in the rivers, and seen the cultivation of the rice. In the fall of the year, the plantation hands, both men and women, work above their knees in water in the rice ditches, pulling out the grass to fit the ground for sowing

B

the rice. Hands sold here from the city find this very severe, having been bred mostly to house labor. The plantations are so deadly that white people cannot remain on them during the Summer time, except at a risk of life. The proprietors and their families are there only through the Winter, and the slaves are left entirely to the overseers. Such overseers as I saw were generally a brutal, gambling, drinking set. I have been to Algiers and seen slavery there. I have seen slavery in Smyrna among the Turks. I was in Smyrna when our American Consul ransomed a beautiful Greek girl in the slave market. I saw her come aboard of the brig " Suffolk," to be sent to America for her education. I have seen slavery in the Spanish and French ports. My opinion is, that American slavery, as I have seen it in the internal slave trade, as I have seen it on the rice and sugar plantations, and in the city of New Orleans, was *full as bad* as any slavery in the world —heathen or Christian. People who go for visits or pleasure through the Southern States, cannot possibly know those things which can be seen of slavery by shipmasters who run up into the back plantations of countries, and who transport the slaves and produce of plantations.

In my past days, the system of slavery was not much discussed. I saw these things as others did, without interference. Because I no longer think it right to see these things in silence, I trade no more south of Mason and Dixon's line.

In 1834, I first saw the *Liberator*. I read it with delight. In July, 1847, I sailed with a loaded vessel bound to Albany, N. Y. On my arrival there, I called on the Mott sisters, ladies well known to the Anti-Slavery friends in Boston and elsewhere. Miss Mott told me they had a slave secreted just out of the city, who was in danger. His name was George Lewis. A writ was out for him, and she wished me to take him to Boston. As soon as I was ready to sail, she brought him to my vessel at night, with his baggage, and I stowed him away. In three days I passed New York, and on getting into Long Island Sound, I told George Lewis he could safely show himself on deck, which he was glad to do.

On the passage, he told me his story. I found him very intelligent for a slave. He had been a Baptist preacher. By trade, he was a house and ship carpenter and bridge builder. He was a slave at City Point, Va., and half-brother to his master, Lewis. He had a wife and seven children, and being entrusted with all the overseeing, often made trips to Washington, where his eldest daughter Lizzie was living with his master's mother. In his absence, the Baptist minister came and took his second daughter from his house for base purposes ; he cried out upon his infamy, and the minister had him hauled up and flogged. George, who had never before been whipped, told his wife he could do nothing more for them, and he must leave them to go to a land of freedom. At night he kneeled down and prayed with them. He then took his saw and a bundle of clothes, and went to the ferry. The ferryman pulled him across James River, and hiding by day, and travelling by the North star at night, he reached the Potomac River, where he found a sloop loaded with wood bound for Alexandria. The captain, knowing him, took him on board, and after dark George made his way over the long bridge to Washington, where his daughter Lizzie hid him in her mistress' attic all Winter. In April, the underground railroad was completed, and he took it for Baltimore, bidding Lizzie good-by, who told him she should soon start herself for a land of freedom. At Baltimore, he was continued on by the same mysterious route to Philadelphia, and so on to New York, where friends forwarded him to the care of the Misses Mott, at Albany. They procured him work, and protected him from the hunters. His master heard of him in this way. When the warm weather came, Lizzie took the same railroad, and followed her father to New York ; there she lost track of him, and the Anti-Slavery friends concluded to send her to Boston. A coast survey steamer came into Boston for repairs. One of the crew, a colored man who had known her in Washington, met her where she was stopping, at Mr. Thacker's in Southac Street, and found out from her that her father was in Albany. He told an officer on board the " Bibb," who was a brother of the master. George Lewis heard of his daughter's being in Boston from the Rev. Mr. Grimes, who was at a meeting near Albany, and said, to the father's great joy, Lizzie was safe in Boston. He also took the news to Lizzie that her father was in Albany. When we reached Boston, Mr. Wallcutt took us to Southac Street, and while we were looking for the number of the house, I heard some one say "Well, there's father!" We turned to look, and it was indeed Lizzie calling "Father!" The next day I took George Lewis to Mr. Samuel Hall's shipyard in East Boston. Mr. Hall employed him for three years. Some of his ship carpenters left on account of it, but Mr. Hall kept George. When George's master found he could not get George back from Albany, he sold his wife and five children to Richmond, Va. The money was raised, and Rev. Mr. Grimes went on to Richmond and bought them, and brought them all to Boston, when George was made a happy man. In 1850, he went to Nova Scotia; he was afraid to stay in Boston after the passage of the Fugitive Slave Law. He staid in Nova Scotia till the Proclamation of Emancipation. His daughter Lizzie is the wife of Mr. Richard S. Brown, of the Boston Custom House, well known as a good citizen, and a credit to his race.

Among the fugitives we had under our care in Boston about the time of Mrs. Stowe's visit, was one woman who had carried her child seven days on her arm in one position. She was nearly paralyzed. Afraid to move or stir, and no room to do so either. The cook stowed her away, and fed her. Clothing in abundance was sent in by the good people from the country for the nearly naked fugitives. I had the care of it in the room over the *Liberator* office.

After the decision was given by U. S. Commissioner Loring that Anthony Burns should be returned to slavery, Wendell Phillips visited him in his cell, and poor Burns looked up into his face with the pathetic appeal, " Mr. Phillips, has everything been done for me that *can* be done? *Must I go back?*" Mr. Phillips said :

"I went over in my own mind the history of Massachusetts. I thought of her schools, her colleges of learning, her churches, her courts, her benevolent and philanthropic institutions, her great names, her Puritans, her Pilgrims, and I was obliged to say, ' Burns, there isn't humanity, there isn't Christianity, there isn't justice enough here to save you ; you must go back.' Then I vowed anew before the ever-living God I would consecrate all the powers He had given me to hasten the time when an innocent man should be safe on the sacred soil of the Puritans."

A month later, the Abolitionists celebrated the Fourth of July at the beautiful grove in Framingham, which must still echo the inspired voices of Garrison, Remond, Thoreau, Pierpont, M. D. Conway, Sojourner Truth, and Phillips, as they kindled Liberty's altar-flames till the bush glowed with her divine presence.

Mr. Phillips pointed out the Summer's work — that would make Massachusetts an Anti-Slavery State. "When it is done, I will be proud of the old Bay State. I used to be proud of her. Time was when I took on my lips the name of the old Commonwealth with a glow of conscious pride that gave depth to the tones of my voice, and an added pulse to the heart. I was proud of her ; but my pride all vanished when I saw that old Indian on her banner go floating down State Street with the Slave Brigade, with Ben Hallett and the U. S. Marshal and a chained slave beneath him. I have lost all pride in Massachusetts till she redeems herself from that second day of June. Let us roll up a petition, a hundred thousand strong, for the removal of Judge Loring."

Mr. Phillips triumphed. "Judge" Loring was "removed." Slave-hunting became odious, and Massachusetts was "redeemed." Burns was sent back to his Virginia owner ; but *he* was the *last*. No fugitive slave was ever seized in Boston and returned after Anthony Burns, in June, 1854. Three years before, Sims had been given up to his doom of slavery in Georgia ; and on the first anniversary of the day, Wendell Phillips said : "Thomas Sims is the first man that the city of Boston ever openly bound and fettered, and sent back to bondage. I have no heart to dwell on so horrible an outrage ; that sad procession in the dim morning through our streets ; the poor youth—his noble effort to break his chains mocked with one short hour of freedom, and then thrust back to the hell he had escaped, by brother man, in the prostituted names of justice and religion. We sit down by the single captive, and weep with him as the iron enters into his soul, too sad to think for the moment of the disgrace of our city, or even the wickedness of its rulers. Pity swallows up indignation. We might be forgiven for the moment if we mistook our sadness for despair. But Liberty knows nothing but victories. In a cause like ours, to which every attribute of the Most High is pledged, ' everything helps us.' Selfish commerce, huckstering politics, and the mocking priest, might turn from such a scene and congratulate each other, saying, ' Our mountain stands strong ;' but we knew emotions were stronger than statutes, more lasting than ledgers, and not to be frozen down even by creeds ; and that all New England would ere long gather itself to answer the last sad question of this hapless victim, as he stepped on the piratical deck of the ' Acorn,'—' Is this Massachusetts liberty ? ' "

That more than a hundred others, who were liable to the same cruel fate of Burns and Sims, *escaped*, was largely due to the tender, watchful devotion of over two hundred noble citizens of Boston, who organized themselves into a Committee of Vigilance under the Higher Law than that of the American Congress — "*Hide the outcast.*" " Betray not him that wandereth." " If the servant escape from his master, he shall dwell with thee in the city that liketh him best." If the throng of memories which the mere sight of this list of members must awaken in every survivor's mind could be stereotyped, what an eloquent volume we should have. The summons, and the hurryings to the rescue ; the scenes in the Court House ; the mass meetings on the Common, in Tremont Temple, in Faneuil Hall ; the speeches, the resolutions, the petitions, the addresses and reports of legislative committees at the State House ; the Personal Liberty Bill ; the sermons of Theodore Parker within " the four thousand peopled walls " of Music Hall ; the cowardly stealing off in the darkest hour before daybreak with Sims to the brig " Acorn " ; Daniel Foster's solemn prayer on Long Wharf ; the pausing of the Vigilance Committee on the spot where Attucks fell, to make fresh resolves to save Massachusetts from another horror like that just witnessed ; the mustering of thousands of Abolitionists, who quit their business, their farms, their shops, their offices, to be the sad *spectators*, if, indeed, they could not be the *rescuers* of Burns ; the tolling of town and village church bells on carrying away the hapless victims, Sims and Burns ; the removal of Judge Loring ; the indignant protests at the setting up of the Daniel Webster statue in the State House Yard ! — how poor and imperfect must be every attempt to preserve that Vigilance Committee's noble work for the decade—1850–1860 — to succor these hunted men, women and children in their extreme peril, so obscure and humble their very names now forgotten, and they floated out like weeds on the great ocean of humanity. Fortunately the Roll of Honor, with the names of the *Vigilance Committee* itself, is in existence, and is now for the first time made public.

It will be seen that talents of every order, from the brightest genius, wit, eloquence, learning, law, divinity, benevolence, wealth, social position, business ability, to those of the humblest pursuits and callings, were volunteered in this angelic, heaven-blessed mission. The printed list has been preserved by me, of which I have the two copies I used — one kept at my desk, and one I carried. I was the doorkeeper of its necessarily guarded meetings held at the Meionaon, the " lesser hall " of the Tremont Temple. It was my business to go round to their places and notify the members when a meeting was called, and I had to stand guard at the door to see that only the right ones went in. There were printed tickets of notice which I delivered to each member in person, if possible, of which the following copies are specimens :

BOSTON, June 7, 1854.

There will be a meeting of the Vigilance Committee at the *Meionaon* (Tremont Temple), on *Thursday Evening*, June 8th, at half past seven.

Pass in by the *Office Entrance*, and through the *Meionaon Ante-Room*.

THEODORE PARKER, *Chairman of Executive Committee.*

VIGILANCE COMMITTEE! — The members of the Vigilance Committee are hereby notified to meet at —— ——

By order of the Committee,

A. BEARSE, *Doorkeeper.*

The Fugitive Slave Law, which the Vigilance Committee meant to resist, defy, baffle and nullify by every possible means, was passed in September, 1850, by the U. S. Congress, and signed by President Fillmore. Humboldt called it the Webster Law. It will be a strange document to the eyes of the new generation that has grown up. Its enactments were in these words: " That any person who shall knowingly and willingly obstruct, hinder, or prevent such claimant, his agent or attorney, or any person lawfully assisting him, her, or them, from arresting such fugitive from service or labor from the custody of such claimant, or shall aid or abet or assist such person directly or indirectly to escape, or shall harbor or conceal such fugitive so as to prevent the discovery and arrest of such person after notice or knowledge of the fact that such person was a fugitive from service or labor, shall for either of said offences be subject to fine and imprisonment."

The Vigilance Committee cheerfully braved the pains and penalties of this infamous law — the six months' imprisonment and one thousand dollar fine for each offence — and obstructed, hindered and prevented, harbored and concealed, with all their mind, might, and soul, *William* and *Ellen Crafts.* Theodore Parker solemnly legalized their marriage, and with his Bible in one hand, and pistol in the other, sent them off to the sheltering folds of England's lion banner, to complete the miracle and romance of their escape.

The first case of actual *arrest* in Boston that fell upon these innocent persons exposed to the slave hounds, was that of

Shadrach, on Saturday morning, Feb. 15, 1851. The warrant was served at the Cornhill Coffee House (late Taft's), Deputy Marshal Riley and an ex-Constable, Byrnes, going there on pretence of getting breakfast; and while Shadrach, a very worthy young man, was unsuspectingly waiting on them, he was seized as the property of U. S. Purser Debree, at Norfolk, Va., and hurried to the Court-room, without even time to put off his waiter's apron. Like a man, he declared that, whatever might be the decree of the Court, he would not be carried to Virginia with breath in his body. Instantly it was noised abroad among his companions and friends that their brother was captured, and was to be sent to perpetual slavery at the South. The excitement spread like wildfire. In a few moments a crowd had assembled around the Court House. Five members of the Boston bar (all members of the Vigilance Committee) volunteered for his defence — Samuel E. Sewall, Charles List, Ellis Gray Loring, R. H. Dana, Jr., and Robert Morris. They obtained a delay to prepare for the defence. At the moment the case was adjourned, a crowd of sympathizing colored persons, at broad noon-day, pressed into the Court-room, surrounded the prisoner, and in the twinkling of an eye, as if operated upon by a sudden electric thrill, fled with him pell-mell from the Court-room, and soon placed him beyond reach of his pursuers. That was a dark, stormy Saturday night, but under its friendly cover. Shadrach started for cold and wintry Canada, to join the 20,000 refugee slaves from the United States — an exile among strangers and poverty.

Mr. Garrison's editorial in the next *Liberator*, "*The Arrest — The Rescue — The Flight*," reads like a psalm of triumphal thanksgiving, a chapter of the Hebrew prophets. "Thank God Shadrach is free! and not only free, but safe under the banner of England. On the Canadian soil he is now standing erect, redeemed and disenthralled, bidding a proud defiance to President Fillmore and all his Cabinet, though backed by the army and navy of the United States. Nobody injured and nobody wronged, but simply a chattel transformed into a man, and conducted to a

c

spot whereon he can glorify God in his body and his spirit which are His. A solitary slave is plucked as a brand from the burning, and forthwith a Cabinet council is held, and the President of the United States is out with a Proclamation of Terror ; conveying it to us in tones of thunder, and on the wings of the lightning, even as though in the Old Bay State chaos had come again, and a million of foreign myrmidons were invading our shores. A poor, hunted, entrapped, fugitive slave is dexterously removed from the court-room, and the whole land is shaken ! A thousand colored seamen of the North may be incarcerated in loathsome cells, and even sold into slavery on the auction block at the South (as many of them are). Official State Commissioners (like Hon. Samuel Hoar), venerable for their years and esteemed for their work, sent to the South to contest the constitutionality of such atrocious acts, are driven away by lawless violence, and not allowed to remain on the soil ; but where is the Presidential Proclamation calling on the people of the South to obey the laws and observe their Constitutional obligations? A hundred free white citizens of the North may be thrown into prison, or tarred and feathered, or compelled to flee for their lives from the South, on suspicion of being morally averse to slavery ; but who cares ? "

Edmund Quincy, with his pen of light, keen satire, wrote the *Liberator's* next editorial —" *Boston on her Knees* " : —

" Times have changed since Boston was the gaze and the admiration of the world for her heroic resistance to tyranny. Seventy years ago she was a little town, in comparison with her present dimensions ; yet she would not submit to insult from the constituted authorities set over her, when they were violating what she esteemed a higher law, and she defied the whole physical force of the most powerful empire in the world, when it presumed to invade her rights. What has been the history of the last fortnight? A man was arrested as a fugitive slave. He was detained, not in the Temple of Justice (as the sycophantic news-papers say, striving to darken counsel with great swelling words of vanity), but in a barracoon — a slave jail — extemporized for

ך

the occasion. The fact that Judge Woodbury sometimes sits in that room is not enough to sanctify it at all other times. When he is on the bench, it is a court-room; when Mr. George T. Curtis (the Little Expounder) sits there as Commissioner, it is a Commissioner's office; when deputy-marshal Riley makes it a place of detention for a fugitive slave, it is a slave jail, and entitled to all the reverence and observance due to a construction for that purpose, and no more. Well, Mr. Slave-Jailer Riley not keeping his jail fast enough, some fifty, or, at the outside, hundred colored men open the door without hurting anybody, and the Boston Shadrach walks quietly out of the jaws of the fiery furnace, which were just yawning for him, body and soul, and goes his way, and is seen no more. Now there is no question these colored men had violated the law of the United States, and were liable to suffer its penalties, if they could be found out. That, we presume, they knew, and had made up their minds to before they undertook the expedition. Just as Hancock and 'the brace of Adamses,' when they undertook to violate the laws of Great Britain, in obedience to the higher law of their generation, knew both what they were doing and the penal consequences of their acts, should they be taken by King George III. The lightning flashes this news to Washington; the Senate resounds with abuse of Boston for several days for this event. The President issues his Proclamation, and the Board of Aldermen and Common Council 'heartily approve' and 'cordially respond, and promise to carry out its recommendations.' We had hardly thought such self-stultification and self-degradation possible even in Websterized Boston. Instead of repelling the Proclamation and its recommendations as insults to Boston, they plump themselves down upon their knees, clap the Firman of the Sultan on their heads, and exclaim, 'Great is Fillmore, and Webster is his prophet! We have deserved it all;' and hold up their cheeks, both sides at once, to be smitten and spit upon. With a coward humility they exclaim, 'We are more ready than ever to do any dirty work you can find for our hands to do!'"

President Fillmore issued a special Proclamation on the third day after Shadrach's rescue — signed by Daniel Webster, his Secretary of State, — directing "prosecution to be commenced against all aiders and abettors of this flagitious offence," and that all who shall be found to have harbored or concealed such fugitive be immediately arrested; and the "dirty work" of arrests was begun with alacrity. First, ELIZUR WRIGHT, of the then *Commonwealth*, for whom Samuel E. Sewall gave bonds, $2,000; CHARLES G. DAVIS, with J. Thomas Stevenson for his bondsman; JAMES SCOTT, and others. On Washington's Birthday, the seventh and eighth arrests were made: LEWIS HAYDEN, for whom bail in $3,000 was promptly given by James N. Buffum, of Lynn, and ROBERT. MORRIS, Esq., for whom Ex-Mayor Quincy, Jr., became bail. The day before, U. S. Marshal Devens purchased sixty revolvers, and distributed them among his men. This fact, when it became known in town, tended rather to excite than quiet public feeling. Arrests continued to be made, and persons held to trial under heavy bonds; all of whom members of the Vigilance Committee were prompt to aid and defend by money, counsel and sympathy.

In this exigency, I was authorized to collect funds, as these interesting autograph letters and signatures show : —

Letter of Mr. Garrison to Theodore Parker.

65 Suffolk Street, March 4, 1851.

ESTEEMED FRIEND :

I understand it has been suggested to the Vigilance Committee that it would be expedient to employ some two or three reliable persons for various purposes — such as obtaining or giving information, collecting funds, &c., &c. — in the present distressing crisis. I think well of the proposition, and would heartily recommend our worthy and faithful friend, AUSTIN BEARSE (with whom you are acquainted), to fill any situation of that kind. Yours, with great regard,

WM. LLOYD GARRISON.

N. B.— God bless you for your many faithful pulpit testimonies.

BOSTON, Oct. 20, 1851.

TO THE FRIENDS OF FREEDOM UNIVERSALLY:

The bearer of this, Capt. AUSTIN BEARSE, has been duly empowered to collect donations to meet the expenses in regard to the rescue cases (still pending) in the affair of Shadrach, and a more trustworthy man could not have been selected for such a purpose. The appeal should at once commend itself to the hearts and pockets of all those who abhor slavery, and who were made glad on hearing of the peaceful deliverance of Shadrach out of the hands of the spoiler. Let every one contribute at least his mite, nor hesitate to make (if it be in his power) a liberal subscription. They who are on trial have claims upon the friends of liberty and justice for their pecuniary co-operation as well as sympathy, and these claims ought to be honored at sight.

WM. LLOYD GARRISON.
WENDELL PHILLIPS.

WASHINGTON STREET, Oct. 19, 1851.

MR. AUSTIN BEARSE:

Dear Sir : I understand that all the money raised for carrying on the defence in the rescue cases has been spent ; also that the money collected for the Vigilance Committee has been nearly spent.

The defendants in the rescue cases are most of them ill able to pay the necessary expenses of resisting the government. No money raised for anti-slavery purposes has been, in my opinion, better spent than what has been used in the rescue trials. As these trials are to come on again immediately, and we have every reason to believe the government will spare no money in its efforts to oppress the prisoners, I trust that you will in the exigency be able to collect all that is necessary to aid in the defence.   Yours truly,

S. E. SEWALL.
ELLIS GRAY LORING.

Also this letter in Mr. Sewall's writing, with autograph signatures of the Committee of Finance : —

The undersigned, Committee of Finance appointed by the Vigilance Committee, hereby certify that AUSTIN BEARSE is authorized to collect subscriptions for the purpose of defraying the expenses incident to the defense of the persons concerned in the rescue of Shadrach.

> W. E. APTHORP,
> S. E. SEWALL,
> ELLIS GRAY LORING,
> J. A. ANDREW,
> WM. W. MARJORAM,
> FRANCIS JACKSON,

May 6, 1851. *Committee of Finance.*

The first subscriptions are : —

Charles Francis Adams, (paid)	-	-	-	$100
S. C. Phillips,	"	-	-	100
Ellis Gray Loring,	"	-	-	25
Wendell Phillips,	"	-	-	100

Acknowledgments by Francis Jackson, treasurer, continued to be made, through the years 1851 and 1852, of donations collected by me in Boston, Lowell, Worcester, &c.— hundreds of dollars — in response to these urgent needs.

Hardly had Shadrach fled the grasp of the slave-hounds, and the excitement cooled, when at night, on the 3d of April, 1851, without a moment's warning, Thomas Sims was seized in Richmond Street, on a lying pretext of theft, by the police, who, disguised as city watchmen, violated the law of Massachusetts that forbade an officer of our commonwealth to aid in arresting a person claimed as a fugitive slave.

Sims made a desperate struggle, wounding a police officer ; but he was overpowered, and smuggled into a carriage, and conveyed into the Court House yard. Not till then did he know he was arrested as a fugitive slave.

As he was taken out, poor Sims was heard to utter a broken sentence to this effect: " I'm in the hands of kidnappers ! " That smothered cry was enough to summon members of the Vigilance Committee. At half past ten o'clock, Theodore Parker,

Elizur Wright and Samuel E. Sewall were in Court Square, demanding of Deputy-Marshal Riley, whom they met, "Is the prisoner to be examined to-night? Tell me at your peril!" and with this, Mr. Sewall, in his earnestness, laid his hand on Mr. Riley. Whereupon the Deputy Riley called on a couple of the numerous "watchmen" so conveniently near, and Mr. Sewall was arrested, and taken to the watch-house. He was soon after released by the Captain of the Watch.

At an early hour next morning heavy chains were found drawn entirely round the Court House, some three or four feet from the ground. The Judges of all the Courts, from Chief Justice Lemuel Shaw down to the lowest official, were obliged to bow down under these chains to perform their high judicial duties. The city police, amounting to sixty men, were constantly employed in guarding the Court House. A regiment of militia was called out and armed. The Courts of the County were no longer open to Massachusetts citizens to enter at their pleasure ; only "gentlemen from the South" were passed in freely by the U. S. Marshal. Sims had escaped from Savannah, Georgia, and was discovered on board the brig "M. C. Gilmore," inside of Boston Light, by the mate, Ames, who was detailed by the owner of the brig to hunt him down in this city. He testified : "I first saw that man in the forecastle. I got a light to see how much chain we had out, when I heard some one say, 'Have we got up?' I was surprised, and said, 'Who are you?' He then laid down, and pretended to be asleep. I took him by the nose, and wrung it for him. * * * It was that nigger there. We put him down into the run, and put the vessel out into the stream. At night we took him into the cabin, because he was most frozen to death, and locked him in. Next morning he was gone — and the boat was gone. He unscrewed the door with his knife, and left the boat at South Boston. He said that nobody but God and himself knew how he came on board."

While Sims was on trial I wrote for the *Liberator:* "I have just had a talk with Ames. I was in hopes he might have been ashamed of his base and inhuman conduct, but he seemed to rather glory in it. ' D— him ! ' he said, ' it was good enough for him.' * * * Trading South transforms men into monsters, but he volunteered to do more than was required. To seize a poor, frozen man and wring his nose, and insult him every way, only because he was endeavoring to free himself from a bondage worse than death, and then to testify against him in court in the worst way he knew how, and, in addition, to boast of it all as he did to me to-day, and to *swear he wished he could do it again,* betrays, to my mind, a heart that few sailors possess. It takes Southern trade, and dealings with Southern slave-holders, to harden any sailor to that extent. Only masters and mates ever get to so bad a pass."

While the trial was proceeding, the Vigilance Committee held meetings to find out which way Sims was to be returned to his master. Russell Marston, S. P. Hanscom, and myself, were detailed to search among the shipping to find any vessel that was preparing to take Sims back to Savannah. The "Acorn" was lying at the end of Long Wharf, and, in my looking around, I found the owners were having a little house built on deck, and I immediately mistrusted the house was to stow away Sims in on the return voyage. I said to Hanscom, "Go down to the vessel and make inquiries about the affair." Mr. Hanscom took a spy-glass and went down, and walks aft, spy-glass in hand, looking down the harbor. At last he got into conversation with the mate, who said, "We've got that d— nigger in close quarters in the Court House," which Hanscom didn't notice, but allowed him to talk on. At last the mate says, "I was the means of his being caught," and told the whole story; pointing to the house, "That's the place we are to put Sims in to take him back to Savannah." Being afraid he had told too much, he turned to Mr. H. with "But, pray, who are you?" Mr. H. replied, "Oh, I'm only a reporter; I've no interest in the matter." That night the Vigilance Committee had a very interesting meeting, and gave me authority to buy a vessel, and follow the "Acorn" out of the harbor, and if possible rescue Sims. But before a vessel could be got ready, the Court decided to send Sims back to his master, and the revenue cutter, anticipating trouble, was sent down with the " Acorn " to Cape Cod.

Charles Sumner, Robert Rantoul, Jr., Charles G. Loring and Samuel E. Sewall interposed all their legal knowledge, and every humane argument, to shield Sims in the court from the fate of slavery; while outside that chained slave-fortress, the noblest pulses of the masses of Boston citizens were stirred to sympathy for the panting heart within the Court House, and roused to righteous indignation that the old State herself was betrayed and dishonored by her officials joining in the mean hunt to drag a fellow being again into the fetters he had broken off in the dear hope of liberty.

A mass meeting was held at a late hour Saturday afternoon on Boston Common, where (as the *Liberator* says) " Wendell Phillips was greeted with hearty cheers as he ascended the steps." His speech, though only "given in substance," ranks with those of Otis and Adams in patriotic fervor, and must hold its due place in the eloquent story of Boston Streets : —

" I should have no doubt of success if we had State courts and Sheriffs disposed to use legal remedies in defence of liberty. One thing is certain ; courts obliged to sit guarded by bayonets will not sit long in Massachusetts. The Commissioner who grants certificates shielded by armed men, will not have many certificates to grant. The law which in this community can only be obeyed at the point of the bayonet cannot stand, ought not to stand, and will not stand long. I rejoice in all this insolent array of force. It is some consolation, however trivial, in this hour of disgrace, that such laws cannot be executed in Boston except by our own officials trampling on the laws of the State, volunteering their illegal services, and by the armed despotism of the Federal Government. This is the first time hostile soldiers have been seen in our streets since the red-coats marched up Long Wharf. May the Government which sends us these earn the same hatred

D

that the masters of the red-coats won! I wish Massachusetts men would crowd our streets, and surround that chained Court House in hundreds of thousands. I would, if this vile deed is to be done, that it should be done in the presence of as many indignant hearts as possible; that they should be obliged, in taking that unhappy man away, to walk over our heads. I know not what others may do, but, for myself, I am resolved if this foul disgrace must come upon our hitherto beloved city, to save for myself the satisfaction of having used all the means that God and nature have put into my hands, in every way my best judgment approves, to preserve her from the stain."

" In accordance with a vote of this mass convention, the Vigilance Committee earnestly urge upon every friend of the slave throughout the Commonwealth, to report himself in Boston on Friday morning, the 11th inst., to witness the last sad scene of the State's disgrace, if it shall be found impossible to avert it. Come by thousands."

Meetings of vast assemblies were held in Tremont Temple during the incarceration of Sims at the Court House, and the most stirring addresses were made or listened to by Dr. Samuel G. Howe, Hon. John G. Palfrey, Horace Mann, Stephen C. Phillips, Hon. Samuel Hoar, Rev. John Pierpont, W. H. Channing, Anson Burlingame, Henry Wilson, C. L. Remond, Elizur Wright and Wendell Phillips. The speech of Mr. Phillips at the close of the State gathering was perfectly electrifying, like that on the Common.

On Sunday, the following request was sent to the clergymen of Boston and vicinity, and in several instances was feelingly complied with: —

The undersigned, a freeman, and in peril, desires the prayers of this congregation that God may deliver him from his oppressor, and restore him to freedom.

his
THOMAS X SIMS.
mark.

Witnesses { S. E. SEWALL.
{ E. W. JACKSON.

Boston, April 5, 1851.

But the sad sequel came. The *Commonwealth* of that date, Saturday, April 12, 1851, announced — *The Victim has been Sacrificed !* —

"Thomas Sims was taken from his prison room in the Court House a few minutes before five o'clock this morning, under the direction of Marshal Tukey, and marched through Court Square, Court and State Streets to the head of Long Wharf, in the centre of a hollow square, and placed on board the brig "Acorn,"— Captain Henry Coombs, of Barnstable, master — and is now on his way to Georgia, and the auction block of slavery. Mayor Bigelow composed part of the escort. As early as half past three o'clock, Marshal Tukey began to muster the men who were to aid him in disgracing Massachusetts, and dooming a young man, a free citizen of Massachusetts, to slavery. The police were armed with U. S. sabres. The slave-guard was drilled for an hour and a half before the final move to the vessel. Sims was brought out of the eastern main entrance of the prison Court House, under the escort of some fifteen men, headed by Marshal Tukey, and marched to the centre of the square mass. As he descended the steps of the Boston barracoon, his sable cheeks were bathed in tears ; and, although he evinced the deepest grief and sorrow, he marched with a firm and manly step, like a martyr and a hero, to his fate. The only demonstration made by the spectators, as the procession passed, were frequent cries of 'Shame! shame!' and questions of 'Is this Boston?' 'Is this Massachusetts?' 'Is that Charlestown and Bunker Hill?' Just as Sims reached the deck of the vessel, a man standing on the wharf cried out, 'Sims ! preach liberty to the slaves !'

"The unfortunate youth was conveyed immediately below, where Cephas J. Ames, the first mate, will be able to execute his fiendish wish, expressed to us on board of that same vessel one week since.

"The instant Sims touched the vessel, the flying jib was hoisted, and the paddles of the tug steamboat, 'Hornet,'—which had been fastened to the brig, in waiting, with steam up, for two hours —

began to move, and at just one minute past five o'clock, the man-stealing craft was gliding down the stream with his victim, amid the hisses and shouts of ' Shame ! shame ! ' from the few lovers of liberty on the wharf.   The whole proceeding was too cowardly to be undertaken under the pale beams of the moon, and so the leader of the work waited until her silver light faded behind the western hills, and then marched with stealthy steps his shameful band over the sacred ground consecrated to liberty and sealed by the blood of our revolutionary fathers.   The only persons who witnessed this crowning disgrace to the soil of Massachusetts were about one hundred of the true and tried members of the Vigilance Committee.   As the ' Acorn ' left the wharf, the vigilant lovers of freedom, who had watched through the night, gathered together, and listened in solemn silence to a tender prayer for the 'poor brother who is carried by force to the land of whips and chains,' by Rev. Daniel Foster.   Then the friends of Sims sang hymns with mournful pathos, and Dr. Bowditch spoke fittingly ; after which the assembly moved up the wharf and street, singing 'Old Hundred,' in its sorely-tried faith : —

' Be thou, O God, exalted high!'

Pausing on the spot in State Street where Attucks fell, the members of the Vigilance Committee resolved to meet at once at the Anti-Slavery office.   Here arrangements were made for various meetings to agitate for the repeal of the Fugitive-Slave bill, or to make it a dead letter.   This notice was sent out : —

' *To the Citizens of Massachusetts :* —

The Committee of Vigilance of Boston, at a meeting held at half past five this morning, passed a resolution respectfully asking the people of Massachusetts to toll the bells in their several towns as the intelligence reaches them of the return of a fugitive slave from this Commonwealth.' "

Several notices of " The Knell of Liberty " appeared in the next *Liberator :* —

" The bells of the Orthodox, Methodist, and Universalist churches of Waltham were tolled on Saturday, when the news of

the man-stealing was received. The bell on the Unitarian church,
being clogged with cotton, would not sound."

"In Newton Upper Falls, the church bells were tolled on Saturday for the removal of Sims."

"The town bell of Plymouth was also tolled on receipt of the
humiliating news."

Mr. Garrison, true to his mighty faith in the eternal Right, said :
"Though a victim has been dragged back to bondage, it will
prove a disastrous triumph to the slave power, and mightily serve
to augment and extend that popular agitation which alone is
needed to effect the utter overthrow of the slave system. We may
be defeated, but our principles never."

And so it proved. The Fugitive-Slave law was brought nearer
home with its affront to every Northern conscience, and set before
each in clearer light the duty to resist its impious demands. It
gave a lever to the Abolitionists, to which Theodore Parker in the
pulpit, Mr. Garrison in the press, Wendell Phillips on the platform, Charles Sumner in the Senate, Henry Wilson in the Free
Soil party, Gerrett Smith in his unceasing, boundless anti-slavery
philanthropy, Whittier in song, Mrs. Stowe in "Uncle Tom's
Cabin," and, finally, old John Brown in Kansas and Harper's
Ferry, all applied such moral might that, at the end of ten years,
the North was prepared to meet the issue in battle, and the final
struggle that upheaved and overthrew the monstrous iniquity of
slavery.

The return of Sims under such difficulties, it would seem, was
no great consolation to Georgia and the South. Jefferson Davis
had said in the debate in the U. S. Senate that followed the
Shadrach rescue, he did not believe the Northern States would
enforce this law. If the mob in Boston was an exposition of the
principles of Massachusetts, he would say to her "Go on!" He
would not enforce her obedience to laws by means of the army
and navy.

A Savannah paper said : —"If our people are obliged to *steal
their property out of Boston in the night*, it would be more profitable

to adopt a regular kidnapping system at once, without regard to law."

The Augusta, Georgia, *Republic* said: "Massachusetts owes to the South the fugitive slaves within her limits; efforts have been made to get several of them back. We lost the two Crafts and Shadrach, and recovered Sims. A faithful execution of the law, indeed! When costs have been subtracted, we should like to know how much has been gained. We shall see. There never was a plainer case in the world. Sims was the fugitive slave of Mr. Potter, beyond dispute; yet the case was kept in court, and before a commissioner, for a whole week. It was necessary to guard him with a heavy police in the third story of the Court House. The building was surrounded by a barricade of chains, and hundreds of the military had to be kept on guard to prevent his forcible rescue. The whole case looks more like a successful farce than anything else. Look at some of the incidents. Mr. Fletcher Webster is imprisoned; Marshal Tukey is held to bail in the sum of a thousand dollars; Mr. Bacon and Mr. De Lyon, the agents of Mr. Potter, were arrested on a charge of conspiracy to kidnap, and had to give bail to the amount of $10,000 — one of the agents narrowly escaped being struck on the head by a negro named Randolph. If his arm had not been caught by an officer, the life of a Southern man would have been sacrificed in an effort to recover a slave under the law of the country. This is the faithful execution of the law! It is the military execution of it. It was the execution of it at great cost and imminent hazard. It was such an execution of it as will prevent nineteen persons out of twenty from attempting to rescue their slaves at all. It would have been impossible for the U. S. Marshal to have resisted the law of the State without the assistance of the municipal authorities of Boston, and the countenance and support of a numerous, wealthy, and powerful body of the citizens. It was in evidence that fifteen hundred of the most wealthy and respectable citizens — merchants, bankers and others — volunteered their services to aid the Marshal."

This fact alone, quoted from report of the State Senate, in the case of Sims, fully justified Mr. Wendell Phillips' indignant rebuke of Boston merchants in a speech of surpassing eloquence, "On the Surrender of Sims," made at the first annual convention of the Massachusetts Anti-Slavery Society held after the return of Sims, Jan. 30, 1852, in Faneuil Hall. Mr. Phillips said: "Who built these walls? Peter Faneuil's ancestors were themselves fugitives from an edict *almost* as cruel as the Fugitive Slave law; and only he whose soul and body refuse to crouch beneath inhuman legislation has a right to be heard here. Nobody else. Daniel Webster did right when he refused to come. A Huguenot built this hall who was not permitted to live on the soil of his own beautiful France, and it may naturally be supposed that he dedicated it to the most ultra, outside idea of liberty. It is a place for the running slave to find shelter — not for the recreant statesman. Times have changed since we were here before. The last time I stood on this platform, there sat beside me a heroine worthy to sit in the hall of the old Huguenot — one Elizabeth Blakesley, a mulatto girl, of Wilmington, North Carolina; who, loving freedom more than slavery, concealed herself on board a Boston brig, in the little narrow passage between the side of the vessel and the partition that formed the cabin — two feet eight inches of room. There she lay while her inhuman master, almost certain she was on board the vessel, called out to her, 'You had better come out! I am going to smoke the vessel!' She tells: 'I heard him call, but my mind was liberty or death.' He smoked the vessel with sulphur and tobacco — three times over. Still she bore it. She came North, half frozen, in the most inclement month of the year — this month. She reached Boston just able to crawl. Where did she come? Oh, those were better times then! She came here. Just able to stand, fresh from that baptism of suffering for liberty, she came *here*. We told her story — and with us that night sat Fredrika Bremer (Charles Sumner was her escort), the representative of the literature of the Old World; and her humane sympathies were moved so much that the rosebud she held in her hand she sent (honoring me by sending it by my hand) to the first representative of American slavery she had seen. It was the tribute of Europe's heart and intellect to a heroine of the black race in Faneuil Hall. Times have changed since. It would not be safe to put Betsey Blakesley on this platform to-night. It would not be safe for her to appear in a public meeting. What has changed this public opinion? I wish it was some single man. I wish it was some official of the city, that so we could make him the scapegoat of public indignation — let him carry it forth, and thus the fair fame of our city be freed.

"This brings me to one of the resolutions I wish to speak of. I think it ought to be read in Faneuil Hall at this, the first, meeting the Abolitionists have held here since the foul deed of April 12th disgraced the city. I feel that these peddling hucksters of State and Milk Streets owe me full atonement for the foul dishonor they have brought on the city of my birth.

"'*Resolved*, that as citizens of Boston and the Commonwealth, we record our deep disapprobation and indignant protest against the surrender of Thomas Sims by the city, its sanction of the cowardly and lying policy of the police, its servile and volunteer zeal in behalf of the man-hunters, and its deliberate wanton and avowed violation of the laws of the Commonwealth for the basest of all purposes — slave-trading ; selling a free man into bondage that State Street and Milk Street might make money.'

"I find but little fault, comparatively, with the City Marshal of Boston, that he did the infamous duty which the merchants of Boston set him. The fault I rather choose to note is, that the owner of the brig 'Acorn' can walk up State Street, and be as honored a man as he was before ; that he walks up our streets as erect as ever; and that no merchant shrinks from his side. But we will put the fact that he owned that brig so blackly on record and the infamous uses he made of it, that his children — *yes, his children* — will, twenty years hence, gladly forego all the wealth he will leave them to blot it out. The time shall come when it will be thought the unkindest thing in the world for any one to remind the son of that man that his father's name was John H. Pearson, and that he owned the 'Acorn.' "

People used to write to Mr. Phillips from the South, out in those places just before slaves were about to start. Mr. Phillips got the letters, and so was on the lookout when the vessels got into Boston harbor. He would know the name of the vessel, and who was on board, and be all ready to help them. Perhaps this was the way little Bernardo came to Bath.

[Letter of Mr. Phillips to Captain Bearse.]

DEAR FRIEND :

When my little colored boy arrives, I wish you to take charge of him, and keep him till you can get some *safe* way to send him to the Cape. You know it is not safe to have colored children travelling about alone, so be very careful that you get him a safe conveyance. He is to be sent to J. E. Mayo, Harwich, to stop at the Union Store there. If Mr. Mayo is not there, Captain Small will attend to him. You must write to Mr. Mayo *two days before he will arrive*, telling him when *to expect him. Pay postage on your letters*. His name is Bernardo. I shall direct the Bath people to have him left at 21 Cornhill. So tell Wallcutt about him, and let him attend to Bernardo till you arrive. *Write me of his arrival the moment he comes.* Charge expenses to me.

Yours truly,   WENDELL PHILLIPS.
January 10, 1853.

CAPTAIN BEARSE :

I have written to have him come by the train that reaches Boston about *one o'clock*. I hope they will be able to send him by that. I suppose some one will be at *the office* at that hour to receive him. Don't let it be locked up.   W. P.

I got the boy safe down to the Cape, as Mr. P. wanted. We used to go to Charles Sumner's house nights. Mr. Sumner and Mr. Phillips, and all, were trying to get Sims out of the hands of the U. S. Marshal with writs, and have him tried, under the laws of Massachusetts, for assaulting a police-officer, etc. I remember

E

Mr. Phillips went with me to counsel about Sims— if there should be such a thing as we could get him off from the " Acorn," going down the harbor, and following after. Mr. Sumner advised having Sims carried right off to Halifax, if he could be rescued.

Members of the Vigilance Committee aided me to money with which I built the yacht " Wild Pigeon," with the purpose to rescue fugitive slaves, who were coming all the while to Boston, as Boston became a noted place of refuge for them. Governor Wise had a pilot boat off the capes of Virginia, that boarded and searched every coasting vessel for fugitive slaves, and made ·each captain pay ten dollars for the search. I intended with the " Wild Pigeon " to go down and resist the pilot boat as a pirate, and appeal to the courts. But the coasting captains would not join me in the enterprise, and it was given up. The " Wild Pigeon " was sold, and the money returned to the gentlemen of the Committee.

Before this, I had the yacht " Moby Dick," and used to take pleasure parties for sailing and fishing down the harbor. It was on the morning of July 15, 1853, the Vigilance Committee heard a slave was on board the brig " Florence " (Captain Amos Hopkins, of Hallowell, Me., from Wilmington, N. C.), anchored off Fort Independence, while the Captain had come ashore for legal assistance. Some colored men on Long Wharf got the story somehow, and, with all speed, William I. Bowditch, Henry Kemp, John W. Browne, and four or five colored men, started with me on the " Moby Dick " down the harbor to look for the brig. We found her, and I rounded up alongside; the mate and crew were on deck. I sent some of the men forward, while Messrs. Bowditch and Browne, with some of the negroes, stood in the boat. I went aft and demanded the negro of the mate; he told me the slave was down in the run. I said roughly, to blind the mate, "I want him, d—— quick!"— and I started for him. He asked if I had the papers all right, and I responded that I had all the papers I wanted, and went down in the cabin and found him. He had slipped off his irons, and I immediately knocked away the shore that held him and he was ready to come. He afterwards said that God told him in the night that somebody would set him free in the morning. I told him to follow me, and he jumped into the boat quick. Mr. Browne said that when he came over the side with his tow dress he looked like Milton's devil. We put for Dorchester bay, and were soon out of sight of the brig and the cutter that lay near her. On the way we had the slave put on other clothes ; it was a fishing suit that belonged to Joseph Southwick ; he kept it on my boat for his own use on fishing excursions. I knew he would be glad to have it used in this cause, for he and his wife Thankful Southwick had always been among the best friends of the fugitive slave. It was in their house George Thompson was safely hid, and from their door that he was taken in a carriage for the English vessel, when his life was hunted in Boston in the mob days of 1835.

Our fugitive in Mr. Southwick's suit could not be told from the other negroes in the boat by a stranger. We landed on the shore, below the City Point House. Mr. King, the landlord, had a horse and carriage standing there, which he let me have — not knowing what I wanted of it. Mr. Bowditch and Mr. Browne took the fugitive in and drove him out to Brookline, and hid him there that night. The next night he was taken to Framingham, and then to Worcester, and so on by the underground railway, to Canada. Some years ago he came back from Canada and visited me, and I have recently learned that he is in Wilmington, N. C. My part in the transaction became known, and it was an injury to me, as many people would not patronize my boat after what I had done.

This is the same rescue of which Theodore Parker said at a celebration of West India Emancipation, held August 1st, 1853, at Framingham : —

"It was proposed yesterday, at Plymouth, (where the anniversary of the Embarkation of the Pilgrims was celebrated,) to build a monument to the memory of the Puritans. It would be a good thing, and he would be glad to see the corner-stone thereof laid, but it would be a little remarkable to erect a monument to those

Pilgrims in a land which was *now* sending out pilgrims who can not hold their rights nor own their own bodies. It was but a fortnight ago, he believed, that the last pilgrim arrived in Massachusetts Bay. He did not come in the 'Mayflower,' but in the brig 'Florence.' He did not come from Delft Haven; he embarked at Wilmington, North Carolina. He did not have Samoset come to him and say, 'Welcome! Englishmen!' The first voice he heard was that of a Yankee sea-captain, and his salutation was after quite another sort. He took him into his boat, and he was spirited away in the darkness of the next night to a land of freedom, beneath the flag of Old England."

One night in September, 1854, Wendell Phillips, Jacob M. Haskell, and J. B. Smith came to my house at nine o'clock, telling me that a schooner lay down at Fort Independence, from Wilmington, North Carolina, with a fugitive slave on board. The schooner proved to be the "Sally Ann," from Belfast, Maine, and was loaded with yellow pine lumber for parties in Boston. They wished me to get my yacht underweigh. I did. Going past the vessel I hailed the schooner and asked the captain if he was ready to give up the slave he had aboard — (having been told by Mr. Haskell that the man to whom the schooner was consigned wanted to get rid of him). The answer I got was this: "If you come alongside my vessel I will send you into eternity —— quick!" So I went on up to Long Wharf and waited for three hours, and only got Mr. Haskell. No other man came. Knowing it was soon coming daylight, I had to lay a plot. I took a dozen old hats and coats and fastened them up to the rail in my yacht, which gave me the appearance of having so many men; I then went down back alongside the schooner again, and told the captain I had now come prepared, and he had better give up the fugitive and save bloodshed. After parleying a little while he agreed to put the slave in my boat. My brother went under his bow with the boat and the slave jumped in, and they pulled alongside the yacht. Then I made sail for City Point, South Boston. I landed the slave and carried him up to my house, stripped off his old tow suit and dressed him in another, so he could not be known. By this time it was daylight. Had just got him ready when Mr. Samuel May, Jr. and Dr. S. Cabot drove up to my house with a carriage, took him and carried him to the Boston and Worcester dépot, and Mr. May went on with him to Worcester, and from there he was sent on the underground railway to Canada.

The next day the vessel hauled into Boston Wharf, and the captain had a notice inserted in the papers that his vessel was boarded by a set of pirates in the night, the slave rescued, and offering $500 for the man who headed the gang. After President Lincoln's proclamation, in 1863, the man returned from Canada and came to see me. He shipped on board a vessel for the West Indies ; I have never seen him since, and cannot recall his name.

The brig "Cameo's" fugitive slave comes next to my remembrance. This was one of those escapes (as I believe) of which Mr. Wendell Phillips had word by letter, and for which he was on the lookout. This is the story, as I lately gave it to the *Traveller :*

In October, 1854, at eleven o'clock, one night, Wendell Phillips, in company with the late Dr. Samuel G. Howe, came to my house at City Point, South Boston, with word that the brig "Cameo," of Augusta, Maine, from Jacksonville, Florida, with a cargo of pine lumber, for Boston, was below. Mr. Phillips also had learned of the secretion of a slave on board, with the intention of gaining his freedom, if possible. Mr. Phillips hearing that the vessel was off Boston Light at sunset the same evening, wished me to get my men together at once, as a part of the Vigilance Committee, and search the city to find the brig. I called my brother, and we both started for the city and summoned the men. I sent some to Charlestown, Chelsea, and East Boston, and some to the North End. I took City Point and Neponset for my route. I gave my brother Boston Wharf as far as Long Wharf, with the intention of examining every vessel lying in the city. The next morning, at eight o'clock, we were to meet at No. 21 Cornhill, which were the headquarters of the Vigilance Committee. At that time and place we met, and my brother had found the brig and slave. The vessel was lying at Boston Wharf. The slave had left the vessel, but the mate followed him and persuaded him to return to it. He had on his slave dress of tow cloth. As soon as possible the Vigilance Committee swore out a writ to search the vessel; and with it in a constable's hand, Mr. Emery B. Fay, Mr. Wendell Phillips, and myself and brother, took a hack and went to Boston Wharf, where the vessel lay. The constable then boarded her and informed the mate that he was about to execute the warrant. The mate in reply told him to go ahead and search. We made a thorough search, but found no slave; but I went down into the after-hatch and there on the lumber was the bed where the slave had rested, during the voyage of twelve days. While I was in the vessel's hold, Mr. Fay called to me to come to him at once. I jumped upon the wharf. He said, "Look at that vessel on the opposite side of the dock; I think the slave we want is there." I went there at once, and as I was getting aboard, the whole crew left, except the slave. The vessel proved to be the schooner "William," of Augusta, Maine, and belonged to the same owners as the "Cameo." The draw-tender was in the act of opening the draw to pass the vessel through. The slave's clothing had been changed, and he was put on board the schooner to go back South to his old master. When I asked him if he was a slave, he looked confused, but made no reply. Again I asked him if he came in the "Cameo,"— pointing to that vessel. He said, "Yes, Massa;" telling me then of the captain's threat to throw him overboard off Cape Cod, if he showed himself. I told him to leave the vessel and follow me, as he was among friends and was now a free man. This he gladly did. Mr. Phillips put him into a carriage, and we drove directly to Lewis Hayden's house, in Southac Street.

The constable returned his writ with the endorsement, "No slave found aboard the 'Cameo.'" Mr. Hayden kept the fugitive about two weeks, when one night, at a meeting of the Vigilance Committee, he informed us that his house was closely watched by a constable and policeman, and he thought it necessary to remove him at once. Accordingly, by agreement, Mr. William I. Bowditch, of Brookline, came with his span of horses to Boston, and he drove to Mr. Hayden's house. Mr. Bowditch opened the carriage door, and the fugitive, dressed in woman's clothes, got in. We then drove down Cambridge Street, over the bridge to East Cambridge, thence to Somerville, from there to Medford, and finally to Concord — arriving at about one o'clock. We drove directly to Mr. Allen's house, by agreement — he being one of the Vigilance Committee. The door was opened, when two men stepped out of the house and took in our lady. We then drove to the tavern, put up our horses and rested until three, A.M., arriving at Brookline at about breakfast time.

The slave was afterwards sent to Canada, where he lived nine years. After the Emancipation Proclamation of 1863, he returned to Boston, joined a colored regiment, went South, and was killed in battle. This slave proved a true patriot by sacrificing his life for his country.

And now we come to the last fugitive slave case in Boston — that of Anthony Burns. To be fully told would require a volume. In what words more true and tender can his story be briefly told than those of Wendell Phillips, in the State House, before the legislative committee in support of the petition to remove Judge Loring, February 20th, 1855? Mr. Garrison said of this argument, delivered in the densely packed halls of the State House: " It is one of those efforts which time makes of historical importance." This is a passage from it, worthy to be learned by every school-child in America :—

" Grant that Burns was Col. Sutter's slave, and what are the facts? A brave, noble man, born unhappily in a Slave State, has shown his fitness for freedom better than most of us have done. At great risk and by great effort obtained he this freedom; but we were only free born. He hides himself in Boston. By hard work he earns his daily bread with patient assiduity ; he sits at the feet of humble teachers, in school and pulpit, and tries to become really a man. The heavens smile over him. He feels that all good men must wish him success in his blameless efforts to make himself more worthy to stand at their side. Weeks roll on, and the heart which stood still with terror at every lifting of the door-latch, begins to grow more calm.

"He has finished his day's work, and under the free stars, wearied, but full of joyful hope that words could never express, he seeks his home, — happy, however humble, as it is his, and it is free. In a moment the cup is dashed from his lips. He is in fetters and a slave ! The dear hope of knowledge, manhood, and worthy christian life, seems gone. To read is a crime, now ; marriage a mockery, and virtue a miracle.

"Who shall describe the horrible despair of that moment ? How the world must have seemed to shut down over him, as a living tomb !

"What hand dealt that terrible blow ? This poor man, against mountain obstacles is struggling to climb up to be more worthy of his immortality. What hand is it that, in this christian land, starts from the cloud and thrusts him back ? It is the hand of one whom your schools have nurtured with their best culture, sitting at ease, surrounded with wealth ; one whom your commission appoints to protect the fatherless and mete out justice between man and man.

"Men ! Christians ! Is there one of you who would for worlds take upon his conscience the guilt of thus crushing a hapless, struggling soul ? Is the man who could, in obedience to any human law, be guilty of such an act, fit to be judge of a Christian people ?

"Mr. Chairman, when you have pronounced on this hasty, reckless, inhuman court its proper judgment, the verdict of official reprobation, you will secure that the next commissioner who opens his court will remember that he opens it in Massachusetts, where a man is not to be robbed of his rights as a human being merely because he is black. You will throw around the unfortunate victim of a cruel law all the protection that Massachusetts incidentally can give. And doing this, you will do something to prevent seeing another such sad week as that of last May or June, in the Commonwealth. If you love Justice or Mercy, you ought to do it."

Theodore Parker said, in his support of the petition : —
" If mindful of your duty to conscience and to God you remove this man from the office, then Massachusetts is clean and noble before the whole United States and the world ; and declares no officer of hers shall ever steal a man, and make his brother a beast of burden. Then you may receive the plaudits of your fellow-men and the approbation of Almighty God."

When the removal came at last, and Massachusetts had set the final seal of her reprobation on her slave-hunting official, the Cape Cod member's fervent "*Amen !*" in the State House was echoed from Barnstable sands to the hills of Berkshire.

> " No slave within her border,
> No slave-hunt on her soil."

www.ingramcontent.com/pod-product-compliance
Lightning Source LLC
Chambersburg PA
CBHW032135080426
42733CB00008B/1088